# Brain Gym®
# *for Business*

## *Instant Brain Boosters for On-the-Job Success*

Gail E. Dennison
Paul E. Dennison, Ph.D.
Jerry V. Teplitz, J.D., Ph.D.

**Edu-Kinesthetics, Inc.**
Ventura, California

Published by Edu-Kinesthetics, Inc., Ventura, California.

Brain Gym® for Business: Instant Brain Boosters for On-the-Job Success
Copyright © 1994 Revised 2000 by Gail E. Dennison,
Paul E. Dennison, Ph.D., and Jerry V. Teplitz, J.D., Ph.D.

Edu-Kinesthetics, Inc.
P. O. Box 3395
Ventura, California  93006-3395  USA
Telephone (805) 650-3303 / Fax (805) 650-1689
email:  EduKBooks@aol.com / www.braingym.com


Inquiries for Jerry Teplitz Enterprises, Inc., should be addressed to:

Jerry Teplitz Enterprises, Inc.
1304 Woodhurst Drive
Virginia Beach, Virginia  23454  USA
Telephone (757) 496-8008 or (800) 777-3529 / Fax (757) 496-9955
email:  Jerry@Teplitz.com / www.Teplitz.com


Brain Gym® is a registered trademark of the Educational Kinesiology Foundation.


Printed in the United States of America


**ISBN 0-942143-03-5**

# Acknowledgments

The authors are grateful to John Thie, D.C., author of *Touch for Health*, for permission to use the frontal eminences (our Positive Points) and the auricular exercise (our Thinking Cap) and to draw from his work our versions of the Brain, Earth, and Space Buttons. This book was written with the help of many dedicated people. Many thanks to Cris Arbo for her illustrations and to Alise Pittman for the book design, layout, typesetting, and cover design. Thanks to Dorothy McKinney and Sonia Nordenson for the many hours of proofreading and editing. Thanks, too, to Dorothy McKinney for additional typesetting. Thanks to Francis Sporer for his artwork. We acknowledge G.C.K. Khalsa for her original compilation of the Seven-Minute Tune-up. Many thanks to Koleen Sargent-Murray for her thoughtful overseeing of this revision, and to Susan Campbell for her typesetting. Finally, the authors wish to thank Lorraine Garnett for her help in the original concept and structuring of this book.

# Contents

# A Message from Dr. Paul Dennison . . .

From the very first time that I offered Brain Gym to the public in 1981, participants have reported greater enjoyment, efficiency, and success in the workplace among the positive results they experienced after taking my workshops. These individuals have spoken of their ability to apply more energy and vitality to their jobs, their improved concentration and productivity when using machines and computers, their increased sales, and their heightened creativity for product development and company management.

Other skills showing equally exciting improvements have included the ability to communicate and get along with people, the ability to be more organized, abilities for public speaking and presentation, increased visual skills, and of course my specialties, reading comprehension and speed-reading.

The work environment itself presents many challenges to the worker: fluorescent lights, computer emanations, and work-flow overloads, to name a few. Some individuals are unusually sensitive to some or all of these influences. Each year, billions of dollars are spent by industry on ergonomics, to design workplaces that are safe from work-related injuries and to make them conducive to fast, economical production. But technology can address only a portion of the problem, for health and productivity ultimately depend upon the individual. There are ways available to each of us to minimize stress in the work environment, and to gain a feeling of personal pleasure each day through the quality of our achievements.

Taking care of our bodies and replenishing our systems with water are simple things that we can do to make the most of our own human potential. The Brain Gym movements serve as the kind of easy and effective self-help tools that we need to optimize our performance and on-the-job satisfaction in the business environment, and it is possible to achieve this optimal performance and satisfaction by doing the movements for just a few minutes each day.

# Introduction

This book offers a series of simple activities designed to minimize stress in the work environment. It will enable you to coordinate your brain functions with your movement skills, allowing you to do your job better, with more ease and enjoyment. Discover this revolutionary approach for yourself!

*Brain Gym® for Business* is easy to use. Just look for your job description in the Job Index listings of the Table of Contents and turn to that page. Under each job description, there is a list of the actual tasks you might be expected to perform. For example, under Secretarial Skills, the list includes "Answering Telephones," followed by specific Brain Gym activities that you can do. The result of doing the activities would be that you would do a better job of answering the phone, would find the work easier, and would feel good, too.

Each Brain Gym activity will take only 30 seconds to one minute to do. By spending four or five minutes on your "Menu," you will feel more ready, willing, and able to "go to work."

To get the most out of your Brain Gym routines, take the time to evaluate your present ability to manage tension. On a scale of 1 to 10, with 1 representing a state of extreme tension and 10, one of ease and relaxation, what is your self-rating as you complete an average day? For example, if you feel somewhat tense, make small errors, or react to criticism negatively, you might assign yourself a 4. Do the Brain Gym activities you have selected for 10 days and then re-evaluate. You will notice an overall improvement as you realize the value of taking care of yourself, the excitement of achieving your daily goals, and the pleasure of improving your skills every day.

# The Importance of Water

Water makes up about the same percentage of our bodies as it does of our planet, approximately 70 percent. And, since our bodies are continually using water, a conscious effort to maintain hydration by replacing lost water is vitally important.

Because water is needed for virtually every biological process, chemical reaction, and mechanical action that takes place in the body, it is crucial to mental and physical performance. As a major component of the blood, water is the delivery system that gets oxygen to each cell of the body. Within the lymphatic system, water carries away waste products as well. It ionizes salts, producing the electrolytes necessary for electrical activity across the cell membranes. It enables us to move our joints and digest our food. Water is essential for the proper use of protein in the body and for the development of the nerve network during learning.

Most people wait until they feel thirsty before drinking water, but thirst lags far behind the body's water needs. If, for instance, you carry out an exercise program and you rely solely on thirst to remind you to replenish water, it may take your body a full 24 hours after each workout to return to proper hydration levels.

Even as you sit and read this page, your body is maintaining a constant, light perspiration, and stress or more strenuous activities increase the amount of perspiration lost. You even lose water (in the form of vapor) every time you exhale! If you live in a typical home you're using still more water, since air-conditioned or heated air robs the body of its normal hydration. On a typical day, two and one-half to three quarts of water are lost by your body. If you exercise for an hour, or if you live in a dry climate, that could add up to another quart.

You can see why we all need to take frequent sips of good-quality water throughout the course of each day. There is surely no simpler, more natural way to both feel better and function better.

# About the Seven-Minute Tune-up

The Seven-Minute Tune-up, described on the following pages, is a simple series of Brain Gym activities that you can do every morning. It's a great way to invest regular time in your most important resource–yourself! This tune-up is an opportunity to easily and successfully begin your day by making sure your brain–in fact, your whole system–gets the blood, oxygen, and electricity it needs. By doing the Seven-Minute Tune-up every day, you will feel better and function better than you ever have before.

Any time during the day that you need an energy boost, or if you feel things are just not clicking, you can do the Tune-up to help you perform to your best potential and to stay in a positive frame of mind.

You can use these seven minutes to review past stresses or potential challenges, and to consider alternative possibilities. This is also a great time to plan your daily (or hourly) schedule, picturing yourself reaching key goals or objectives. Many people tell us that choosing an activity or two from the Tune-up whenever they are under emotional stress, or have a critical decision to make, helps them to increase their productive hours and days.

# The Seven-Minute Tune-up

### 1. Water
Sip some water.
(See page iv)

### 2. Belly Breathing
Take 4 - 8 complete
breaths. (See page 34)

### 3. Brain Buttons
Look right and left as you
massage the points for
4 - 8 breaths. (See page 35)

### 4. Hook-ups

#### Part 1
Relax for 4-8 breaths. Additionally, you
may want to review areas of stress and
consider alternative possibilities.
(See page 46)

### Part 2
Place fingertips together and feet flat on
floor for another 4-8 complete breaths.
(See page 47)

## 5. Brain-Integration Movement
Extend your arms out as wide apart
as is comfortable. Picture bringing your
left and right brain hemispheres together,
as you bring your two hands together,
interlocking your fingers. Enjoy this
connection for 4-8 breaths.

## 6. Positive Points
Hold the points lightly for 4-8 breaths.
You might use this time to plan your day.
(See page 51)

## 7. Cross Crawl
Move into action as you complete the Tune-up
with 10-25 repetitions of Cross Crawl.
(See page 37)

# Job Index

Find your job title(s) among the following pages. Scan the requisite tasks listed in bold on the left side of each page and select any that you would like to improve at this time. Do the recommended menu of Brain Gym Activities (described in detail on pages 29 - 55) just prior to or interspersed with each task, as appropriate. As you complete your menu, acknowledge yourself for any improvement you notice in the level of comfort, ease, or enjoyment of your work, or in the effectiveness of your job performance.

(If you cannot find your job title, or for additional tasks, see the Task Index on page 23. The Task Index lists all the work skills you need to put together your own customized Brain Gym program.)

# Accounting

**Using Math Skills** - Earth Buttons, Space Buttons, Balance Buttons, The Thinking Cap, The Owl, The Energy Yawn

**Interpreting Legal Codes and Language** - Brain Buttons, Earth Buttons, Lazy 8s, Positive Points

**Working in Columns** - Brain Buttons, The Cross Crawl, Earth Buttons, Space Buttons, Lazy 8s

**Paying Attention to Detail** - Brain Buttons, The Cross Crawl, Earth Buttons, Lazy 8s

**Focusing Attention** - The Calf Pump, The Footflex, The Gravity Glider, The Owl

**Spelling with Accuracy** - Earth Buttons, The Elephant, The Thinking Cap, The Owl

**Following Through** - Hook-ups, The Energy Yawn, The Footflex, The Calf Pump

**Filling Out Forms -** Arm Activation, The Double Doodle, Alphabet 8s, The Energy Yawn

**Organizing Paperwork** - The Double Doodle, The Rocker, Positive Points

**Staying on Schedule** - Belly Breathing, Earth Buttons, Balance Buttons, Positive Points, Hook-ups

**Sitting Comfortably** - Arm Activation, The Grounder, The Gravity Glider, The Cross Crawl (the seated variation)

**Inputting with Accuracy** - Brain Buttons, Balance Buttons, Earth Buttons, The Thinking Cap

**Being Comfortable at the Computer** - Water, Brain Buttons, Balance Buttons, Neck Rolls, Hook-ups

**Comfort Working Alone** - Water, Brain Buttons, The Cross Crawl, Hook-ups

**Communicating Effectively** - The Calf Pump, The Footflex, Lazy 8s, The Energy Yawn

**Communicating with Clients** - The Energy Yawn, The Footflex, The Calf Pump, The Gravity Glider

**Maintaining Confidence** - Balance Buttons, Earth Buttons, Space Buttons

**Listening Actively and Attentively** - The Thinking Cap, The Elephant, The Owl

**Accessing Memory** - The Elephant, The Owl, The Thinking Cap

**Seeing Other Points of View -** The Calf Pump, The Footflex, Hook-ups

**Maintaining Positive Energy -** Positive Points, Hook-ups, Balance Buttons

**Keeping a Sense of Humor** - The Rocker, Arm Activation, The Thinking Cap, The Energy Yawn, Hook-ups

**Carrying Out Instructions** - The Thinking Cap, Balance Buttons, The Owl, The Elephant, The Cross Crawl, Hook-ups

**Leaving Voice Mail Messages** - Hook-ups, The Energy Yawn, The Calf Pump, The Energizer

**Surfing the Internet** - The Cross Crawl, Brain Buttons, The Thinking Cap, Arm Activation

# Administrative Assistance

**Communicating Effectively** - The Calf Pump, The Footflex, Lazy 8s,
The Energy Yawn

**Maintaining Comfort with People** - The Calf Pump, The Footflex,
The Energy Yawn, The Energizer

**Working as Part of a Team** - The Double Doodle, The Footflex, The Calf Pump

**Maintaining Confidence** - Balance Buttons, Earth Buttons, Space Buttons

**Listening Actively and Attentively** - The Thinking Cap, The Elephant, The Owl

**Accessing Memory** - The Elephant, The Owl, The Thinking Cap

**Seeing Other Points of View** - The Calf Pump, The Footflex, Hook-ups

**Maintaining Positive Energy** - Positive Points, Hook-ups, Balance Buttons

**Focusing Attention** - The Calf Pump, The Footflex, The Gravity Glider, The Owl

**Keeping a Sense of Humor** - The Rocker, Arm Activation, The Thinking Cap,
The Energy Yawn, Hook-ups

**Handling Complaints** - The Footflex, The Gravity Glider, The Calf Pump

**Handling Criticism** - The Calf Pump, Hook-ups, Positive Points

**Paying Attention to Detail** - Brain Buttons, The Cross Crawl, Earth Buttons, Lazy 8s

**Filing** - Balance Buttons, Earth Buttons, Space Buttons

**Carrying Out Instructions** - The Thinking Cap, Balance Buttons, The Owl,
The Elephant, The Cross Crawl, Hook-ups

**Staying on Schedule** - Belly Breathing, Earth Buttons, Balance Buttons,
Positive Points, Hook-ups

**Organizing Bulk Mailings** - Water, The Grounder, The Cross Crawl, Think of an X

**Organizing and Completing Errands** - The Thinking Cap, Lazy 8s,
The Cross Crawl

**Reading without Eyestrain** - Water, Brain Buttons, Earth Buttons, Lazy 8s,
The Cross Crawl, Think of an X

**Being Comfortable at the Computer** - Water, Brain Buttons, Balance Buttons,
Neck Rolls, Hook-ups

**Maintaining Versatility** - The Footflex, The Rocker, The Cross Crawl (the seated variation), The Energizer

**Writing Legibly** - Arm Activation, The Double Doodle, Lazy 8s, Alphabet 8s

**Reading with Comprehension** - The Footflex, The Gravity Glider, The Grounder, The Calf Pump

**Speed-Reading** - The Calf Pump, The Cross Crawl, Lazy 8s, Think of an X

**Spelling with Accuracy** - Earth Buttons, The Elephant, The Thinking Cap, The Owl

**Driving with Comfort** - Balance Buttons, Lazy 8s, Hook-ups, Positive Points

**Leaving Voice Mail Messages** - Hook-ups, The Energy Yawn, The Calf Pump, The Energizer

**Surfing the Internet** - The Cross Crawl, Brain Buttons, The Thinking Cap, Arm Activation

# Computer Programming

**Sitting Comfortably** - Arm Activation, The Grounder, The Gravity Glider,
        The Cross Crawl (the seated variation)

**Being Comfortable at the Computer** - Water, Brain Buttons, Balance Buttons,
        Neck Rolls, Hook-ups

**Accessing Creativity** - The Double Doodle, The Footflex, The Calf Pump,
        The Energy Yawn

**Preventing Eyestrain at the Computer** - Water, Brain Buttons, The Cross Crawl,
        Lazy 8s

**Coordinating Processes at the Keyboard** - Arm Activation, The Double Doodle,
        Lazy 8s, Alphabet 8s

**Maintaining Postural Flexibility** - Arm Activation, The Cross Crawl,
        The Gravity Glider, The Energizer

**Focusing Attention** - The Calf Pump, The Footflex, The Gravity Glider, The Owl

**Inputting with Accuracy** - Brain Buttons, Balance Buttons, Earth Buttons,
        The Thinking Cap

**Entering Data with Speed, Accuracy, and Comfort** - Water, Brain Buttons,
        Neck Rolls, Hook-ups

**Paying Attention to Detail** - Brain Buttons, The Cross Crawl, Earth Buttons, Lazy 8s

**Staying Calm** - Earth Buttons, Hook-ups, Positive Points

**Problem Solving** - The Cross Crawl, Balance Buttons, Neck Rolls, Positive Points

**Maximizing Programming Abilities** - The Calf Pump, The Elephant,
        Neck Rolls, The Owl

**Troubleshooting Hardware and Software Problems** - Earth Buttons,
        Space Buttons, The Energizer, Hook-ups

**Staying on Schedule** - Belly Breathing, Earth Buttons, Balance Buttons,
        Positive Points, Hook-ups

**Comfort Working Alone** - Water, Brain Buttons, The Cross Crawl, Hook-ups

**Following Up** - The Rocker, The Energizer, The Cross Crawl

**Planning Long-Range Strategies** - The Calf Pump, The Grounder,
The Gravity Glider, The Elephant

**Maintaining Positive Energy** - Positive Points, Hook-ups, Balance Buttons

**Surfing the Internet** - The Cross Crawl, Brain Buttons, The Thinking Cap,
Arm Activation

# Customer Service

**Projecting Confidence** - The Thinking Cap, The Owl, The Cross Crawl, Positive Points

**Developing Rapport** - The Footflex, The Energy Yawn, Lazy 8s, The Calf Pump

**Maintaining Comfort with People** - The Calf Pump, The Footflex, The Energy Yawn, The Energizer

**Maintaining Positive Energy** - Positive Points, Hook-ups, Balance Buttons

**Handling Complaints** - The Footflex, The Gravity Glider, The Calf Pump

**Handling Rejection** - Belly Breathing, Neck Rolls, The Energy Yawn, Positive Points, Hook-ups

**Maintaining Self-Control** - Balance Buttons, Hook-ups, Positive Points

**Keeping a Sense of Humor** - The Rocker, Arm Activation, The Thinking Cap, The Energy Yawn, Hook-ups

**Maintaining Telephone Voice Quality** - The Elephant, The Energy Yawn, The Owl, The Thinking Cap, Hook-ups

**Feeling Comfortable on the Telephone** - Balance Buttons, The Elephant, The Owl, Arm Activation, The Energy Yawn, The Thinking Cap

**Writing Legibly** - Arm Activation, The Double Doodle, Lazy 8s, Alphabet 8s

**Leaving Voice Mail Messages** - Hook-ups, The Energy Yawn, The Calf Pump, The Energizer

# Data Processing

**Sitting Comfortably** - Arm Activation, The Grounder, The Gravity Glider, The Cross Crawl (the seated variation)

**Being Comfortable at the Computer** - Water, Brain Buttons, Balance Buttons, Neck Rolls, Hook-ups

**Sequencing Numbers with Precision** - The Calf Pump, The Elephant, Neck Rolls, The Owl, The Gravity Glider, The Double Doodle

**Entering Data with Speed, Accuracy, and Comfort** - Water, Brain Buttons, Neck Rolls, Hook-ups

**Coordinating Processes at the Keyboard** - Arm Activation, The Double Doodle, Lazy 8s, Alphabet 8s

**Preventing Eyestrain at the Computer** - Water, Brain Buttons, The Cross Crawl, Lazy 8s

**Working with Lists on the Computer** - Earth Buttons, Space Buttons, Balance Buttons

**Inputting with Accuracy** - Brain Buttons, Balance Buttons, Earth Buttons, The Thinking Cap

**Spelling with Accuracy** - Earth Buttons, The Elephant, The Thinking Cap, The Owl

**Maintaining Enthusiasm** - Hook-ups, The Calf Pump, The Gravity Glider

# Management

**Setting Priorities** - Space Buttons, The Thinking Cap, The Cross Crawl, Hook-ups

**Maintaining Positive Energy** - Positive Points, Hook-ups, Balance Buttons

**Accessing Creativity** - The Double Doodle, The Footflex, The Calf Pump, The Energy Yawn

**Handling Personnel Decisions** - The Footflex, The Grounder, The Calf Pump, The Gravity Glider

**Expressing Leadership Skills** - The Footflex, The Calf Pump, The Energy Yawn, Lazy 8s

**Delegating Responsibility** - The Grounder, The Gravity Glider, The Owl

**Planning Long-Range Strategies** - The Calf Pump, The Grounder, The Gravity Glider, The Elephant

**Meeting Quotas** - Earth Buttons, Space Buttons, Balance Buttons

**Modeling Good Co-Worker Relations** - The Cross Crawl, The Rocker, Neck Rolls, The Energy Yawn, Belly Breathing

**Team-Building** - The Rocker, The Calf Pump, Balance Buttons, The Cross Crawl, Lazy 8s

**Giving Constructive Criticism** - Neck Rolls, The Energy Yawn, Belly Breathing

**Keeping a Sense of Humor** - The Rocker, Arm Activation, The Thinking Cap, The Energy Yawn, Hook-ups

**Handling Criticism** - The Calf Pump, Hook-ups, Positive Points

**Managing Resources** - Balance Buttons, Earth Buttons, Space Buttons

**Conducting Interviews** - The Footflex, The Calf Pump, The Energy Yawn, Lazy 8s

**Public Speaking** - The Elephant, The Owl, The Energy Yawn, The Thinking Cap, The Cross Crawl, Hook-ups, Positive Points

**Reading with Comprehension** - The Footflex, The Gravity Glider, The Grounder, The Calf Pump

**Reading Aloud** - The Rocker, Neck Rolls, The Energy Yawn, Belly Breathing

**Speed-Reading** - The Calf Pump, The Cross Crawl, Lazy 8s, Think of an X

**Effective Writing** - The Calf Pump, The Footflex, The Owl, The Energy Yawn

**Setting and Meeting Goals** - Water, Brain Buttons, The Cross Crawl, Hook-ups

**Holding to Values -** The Calf Pump, The Footflex, The Energy Yawn, Hook-ups

**Leading Meetings -** The Calf Pump, Brain Buttons, Balance Buttons, Hook-ups

**Leaving Voice Mail Messages** - Hook-ups, The Energy Yawn, The Calf Pump, The Energizer

**Surfing the Internet** - The Cross Crawl, Brain Buttons, The Thinking Cap, Arm Activation

# Public Relations

**Accessing Positive Self-Concept** - Positive Points, Hook-ups, Balance Buttons

**Accessing Memory** - The Elephant, The Owl, The Thinking Cap

**Appreciating Your Own Appearance** - Earth Buttons, Space Buttons, Balance Buttons

**Projecting Confidence** - The Thinking Cap, The Owl, The Cross Crawl, Positive Points

**Staying Calm** - Earth Buttons, Hook-ups, Positive Points

**Feeling Comfortable on the Telephone** - Balance Buttons, The Elephant, The Owl, Arm Activation, The Energy Yawn, The Thinking Cap

**Maintaining Telephone Voice Quality** - The Elephant, The Energy Yawn, The Owl, The Thinking Cap, Hook-ups

**Maintaining Comfort with People** - The Calf Pump, The Footflex, The Energy Yawn, The Energizer

**Keeping a Sense of Humor** - The Rocker, Arm Activation, The Thinking Cap, The Energy Yawn, Hook-ups

**Effective Writing** - The Calf Pump, The Footflex, The Owl, The Energy Yawn

**Being Comfortable at the Computer** - Water, Brain Buttons, Balance Buttons, Neck Rolls, Hook-ups

**Keyboarding with Dexterity** - Brain Buttons, Balance Buttons, Earth Buttons, Arm Activation, The Double Doodle, Lazy 8s

**Handling Multiple Tasks** - Brain Buttons, The Grounder, Hook-ups

**Leaving Voice Mail Messages** - Hook-ups, The Energy Yawn, The Calf Pump, The Energizer

**Surfing the Internet** - The Cross Crawl, Brain Buttons, The Thinking Cap, Arm Activation

# Sales

**Cold Calling** - Positive Points, The Thinking Cap, The Owl, The Cross Crawl

**Developing Rapport** - The Footflex, The Energy Yawn, Lazy 8s, The Calf Pump

**Comfort Working Alone** - Water, Brain Buttons, The Cross Crawl, Hook-ups

**Working as Part of a Team** - The Double Doodle, The Footflex, The Calf Pump

**Driving with Comfort** - Balance Buttons, Lazy 8s, Hook-ups, Positive Points

**Comfortable Air Travel** - Balance Buttons, The Elephant, Lazy 8s, The Cross Crawl, Hook-ups, Positive Points

**Maintaining Comfort with People** - The Calf Pump, The Footflex, The Energy Yawn, The Energizer

**Maintaining Positive Energy** - Positive Points, Hook-ups, Balance Buttons

**Filling Out Repetitive Paperwork** - Brain Buttons, Earth Buttons, Arm Activation, Lazy 8s, Alphabet 8s

**Maintaining Postural Flexibility** - Arm Activation, The Cross Crawl, The Gravity Glider, The Energizer

**Following Up** - The Rocker, The Energizer, The Cross Crawl

**Writing Legibly** - Arm Activation, The Double Doodle, Lazy 8s, Alphabet 8s

**Effective Writing** - The Calf Pump, The Footflex, The Owl, The Energy Yawn

**Answering Telephones** - The Thinking Cap, The Elephant, The Owl

**Leaving Voice Mail Messages** - Hook-ups, The Energy Yawn, The Calf Pump, The Energizer

**Being Comfortable at the Computer** - Water, Brain Buttons, Balance Buttons, Neck Rolls, Hook-ups

**Keyboarding with Dexterity** - Brain Buttons, Balance Buttons, Earth Buttons, Arm Activation, The Double Doodle, Lazy 8s

**Surfing the Internet** - The Cross Crawl, Brain Buttons, The Thinking Cap, Arm Activation

# Secretarial Skills

**Listening Actively and Attentively** - The Thinking Cap, The Elephant, The Owl

**Organizing Paperwork** - Double Doodle, The Rocker, Positive Points

**Speaking Clearly** - The Energy Yawn, The Thinking Cap, The Elephant, Hook-ups

**Maintaining Positive Energy** - Positive Points, Hook-ups, Balance Buttons

**Setting Priorities** - Space Buttons, The Thinking Cap, The Cross Crawl, Hook-ups

**Handling Criticism** - The Calf Pump, Hook-ups, Positive Points

**Answering Telephones** - The Thinking Cap, The Elephant, The Owl

**Maintaining Telephone Voice Quality** - The Elephant, The Energy Yawn, The Owl, The Thinking Cap, Hook-ups

**Sitting Comfortably -** Arm Activation, The Grounder, The Gravity Glider, The Cross Crawl (the seated variation)

**Maintaining Postural Flexibility** - Arm Activation, The Cross Crawl, The Gravity Glider, The Energizer

**Composing Letters** - The Calf Pump, The Footflex, The Owl, The Energy Yawn

**Writing Legibly** - Arm Activation, The Double Doodle, Lazy 8s, Alphabet 8s

**Reading with Comprehension** - The Footflex, The Gravity Glider, The Grounder, The Calf Pump

**Reading without Eyestrain** - Water, Brain Buttons, Earth Buttons, Lazy 8s, The Cross Crawl, Think of an X

**Spelling with Accuracy** - Earth Buttons, The Elephant, The Thinking Cap, The Owl

**Carrying Out Instructions** - The Thinking Cap, Balance Buttons, The Owl, The Elephant, The Cross Crawl, Hook-ups

**Using Math Skills** - Earth Buttons, Space Buttons, Balance Buttons, The Thinking Cap, The Owl, The Energy Yawn

**Filing** - Balance Buttons, Earth Buttons, Space Buttons

**Maintaining Inventory and Supplies** - The Cross Crawl, The Grounder, The Gravity Glider, The Owl, The Energizer

**Handling Criticism** - The Calf Pump, Hook-ups, Positive Points

**Being Assertive** - Balance Buttons, Hook-ups, Positive Points

**Being Comfortable at the Computer** - Water, Brain Buttons, Balance Buttons, Neck Rolls, Hook-ups

**Coordinating Processes at the Keyboard** - Arm Activation, The Double Doodle, Lazy 8s, Alphabet 8s

**Staying on Schedule** - Belly Breathing, Earth Buttons, Balance Buttons, Positive Points, Hook-ups

**Leaving Voice Mail Messages** - Hook-ups, The Energy Yawn, The Calf Pump, The Energizer

**Surfing the Internet** - The Cross Crawl, Brain Buttons, The Thinking Cap, Arm Activation

# Shipping and Receiving

**Maintaining Postural Flexibility** - Arm Activation, The Cross Crawl,
The Gravity Glider, The Energizer

**Packing and Categorizing Boxes** - The Grounder, The Gravity Glider,
Brain Buttons, Earth Buttons, Space Buttons

**Coordinating Invoices and Products -** Balance Buttons, The Owl, The Cross Crawl,
Lazy 8s

**Maintaining Inventory and Supplies -** The Cross Crawl, The Grounder,
The Gravity Glider, The Owl, The Energizer

**Maintaining Positive Energy** - Positive Points, Hook-ups, Balance Buttons

**Handling Multiple Tasks** - Brain Buttons, The Grounder, Hook-ups

**Following Up** - The Rocker, The Energizer, The Cross Crawl

**Sitting Comfortably** - Arm Activation, The Grounder, The Gravity Glider,
The Cross Crawl (the seated variation)

**Being Comfortable at the Computer** - Water, Brain Buttons, Balance Buttons,
Neck Rolls, Hook-ups

**Keyboarding with Dexterity** - Brain Buttons, Balance Buttons, Earth Buttons,
Arm Activation, The Double Doodle, Lazy 8s

**Operating ATM Machines** - Water, Brain Buttons, Earth Buttons, Space Buttons,
Lazy 8s

**Staying on Schedule** - Belly Breathing, Earth Buttons, Balance Buttons,
Positive Points, Hook-ups

**Reading with Accuracy** - Water, Brain Buttons, Earth Buttons, Lazy 8s,
The Cross Crawl

**Using Math Skills** - Earth Buttons, Space Buttons, Balance Buttons,
The Thinking Cap, The Owl, The Energy Yawn

**Spelling with Accuracy** - Earth Buttons, The Elephant, The Thinking Cap,
The Owl

**Paying Attention to Detail** - Brain Buttons, The Cross Crawl, Earth Buttons, Lazy 8s

**Filling Out Repetitive Paperwork** - Brain Buttons, Earth Buttons, Arm Activation,
Lazy 8s, Alphabet 8s

**Organizing Paperwork** - The Double Doodle, The Rocker, Positive Points

**Carrying Out Instructions** - The Thinking Cap, Balance Buttons, The Owl, The Elephant, The Cross Crawl, Hook-ups

**Feeling Comfortable on the Telephone** - Balance Buttons, The Elephant, The Owl, Arm Activation, The Energy Yawn, The Thinking Cap

**Driving with Comfort** - Balance Buttons, Lazy 8s, Hook-ups, Positive Points

# Supervising

**Maintaining Positive Energy** - Positive Points, Hook-ups, Balance Buttons

**Holding to Objectives** - Balance Buttons, Hook-ups, Positive Points

**Communicating Effectively** - The Calf Pump, The Footflex, Lazy 8s,
        The Energy Yawn

**Seeing Other Points of View** - The Calf Pump, The Footflex, Hook-ups

**Using Tact** - The Calf Pump, The Grounder, The Gravity Glider, The Footflex

**Delegating Responsibility** - The Grounder, The Gravity Glider, The Owl

**Setting Limits** - Positive Points, Hook-ups, Balance Buttons

**Giving Constructive Criticism -** Neck Rolls, The Energy Yawn, Belly Breathing

**Handling Personnel Decisions -** The Footflex, The Grounder, The Calf Pump,
        The Gravity Glider

**Meeting Quotas** - Earth Buttons, Space Buttons, Balance Buttons

**Taking Responsibility** - Positive Points, Think of an X, Belly Breathing

**Maintaining Postural Flexibility** - Arm Activation, The Cross Crawl,
        The Gravity Glider, The Energizer

**Writing Legibly** - Arm Activation, The Double Doodle, Lazy 8s, Alphabet 8s

**Reading without Eyestrain** - Water, Brain Buttons, Earth Buttons, Lazy 8s,
        The Cross Crawl, Think of an X

**Reading with Comprehension** - The Footflex, The Gravity Glider,
        The Grounder, The Calf Pump

**Staying on Schedule** - Belly Breathing, Earth Buttons, Balance Buttons,
        Positive Points, Hook-ups

**Leaving Voice Mail Messages** - Hook-ups, The Energy Yawn, The Calf Pump,
        The Energizer

**Surfing the Internet** - The Cross Crawl, Brain Buttons, The Thinking Cap,
        Arm Activation

# Technical Skills

**Sitting Comfortably** - Arm Activation, The Grounder, The Gravity Glider, The Cross Crawl (the seated variation)

**Being Comfortable at the Computer** - Water, Brain Buttons, Balance Buttons, Neck Rolls, Hook-ups

**Coordinating Processes at the Keyboard** - Arm Activation, The Double Doodle, Lazy 8s, Alphabet 8s

**Accessing Memory** - The Elephant, The Owl, The Thinking Cap

**Using Mechanical Skills** - Brain Buttons, Arm Activation, The Cross Crawl

**Maintaining Confidence** - Balance Buttons, Earth Buttons, Space Buttons

**Keeping a Sense of Humor** - The Rocker, Arm Activation, The Thinking Cap, The Energy Yawn, Hook-ups

**Troubleshooting of Equipment Problems** - Earth Buttons, Space Buttons, The Energizer, Hook-ups

**Reading without Eyestrain** - Water, Brain Buttons, Earth Buttons, Lazy 8s, The Cross Crawl, Think of an X

**Inputting with Accuracy** - Brain Buttons, Balance Buttons, Earth Buttons, The Thinking Cap

**Effective Writing** - The Calf Pump, The Footflex, The Owl, The Energy Yawn

**Maintaining Postural Flexibility** - Arm Activation, The Cross Crawl, The Gravity Glider, The Energizer

**Staying on Schedule** - Belly Breathing, Earth Buttons, Balance Buttons, Positive Points, Hook-ups

**Leaving Voice Mail Messages** - Hook-ups, The Energy Yawn, The Calf Pump, The Energizer

**Surfing the Internet** - The Cross Crawl, Brain Buttons, The Thinking Cap, Arm Activation

# Telemarketing

**Sitting Comfortably** - Arm Activation, The Grounder, The Gravity Glider, The Cross Crawl (the seated variation)

**Answering Telephones** - The Thinking Cap, The Elephant, The Owl

**Feeling Comfortable on the Telephone** - Balance Buttons, The Elephant, The Owl, Arm Activation, The Energy Yawn, The Thinking Cap

**Maintaining Telephone Voice Quality** - The Elephant, The Energy Yawn, The Owl, The Thinking Cap, Hook-ups

**Listening Actively and Attentively** - The Thinking Cap, The Elephant, The Owl

**Answering Questions** - The Calf Pump, The Grounder, The Footflex

**Cold Calling** - Positive Points, The Thinking Cap, The Owl, The Cross Crawl

**Being Assertive** - Balance Buttons, Hook-ups, Positive Points

**Developing Rapport** - The Footflex, The Energy Yawn, Lazy 8s, The Calf Pump

**Dealing with Disappointment** - Positive Points, Hook-ups

**Seeing Other Points of View** - The Calf Pump, The Footflex, Hook-ups

**Following Up** - The Rocker, The Energizer, The Cross Crawl

**Memorizing a Script** - The Owl, The Elephant, The Energy Yawn, The Thinking Cap

**Remembering Product Knowledge** - Balance Buttons, Neck Rolls, The Cross Crawl, Positive Points

**Handling Objections Calmly** - The Energy Yawn, Neck Rolls, Belly Breathing

**Handling Rejection** - Belly Breathing, Neck Rolls, The Energy Yawn, Positive Points, Hook-ups

**Keeping a Sense of Humor** - The Rocker, Arm Activation, The Thinking Cap, The Energy Yawn, Hook-ups

**Setting and Meeting Goals** - Water, Brain Buttons, The Cross Crawl, Hook-ups

**Maintaining Comfort with People** - The Calf Pump, The Footflex, Lazy 8s, The Energy Yawn, The Energizer

**Maintaining Positive Energy** - Positive Points, Hook-ups, Balance Buttons

**Paying Attention to Detail** - Brain Buttons, The Cross Crawl, Earth Buttons, Lazy 8s

**Organizing Paperwork** - The Double Doodle, The Rocker, Positive Points

**Filling Out Repetitive Paperwork** - Brain Buttons, Earth Buttons, Arm Activation, Lazy 8s, Alphabet 8s

**Maintaining Postural Flexibility** - Arm Activation, The Cross Crawl, The Gravity Glider, The Energizer

**Leaving Voice Mail Messages** - Hook-ups, The Energy Yawn, The Calf Pump, The Energizer

# Writing, Editing, Proofreading

**Accessing Creativity** - The Double Doodle, The Footflex, The Calf Pump, The Energy Yawn

**Effective Writing -** The Calf Pump, The Footflex, The Owl, The Energy Yawn

**Writing Legibly -** Arm Activation, The Double Doodle, Lazy 8s, Alphabet 8s

**Sitting Comfortably** - Arm Activation, The Grounder, The Gravity Glider, The Cross Crawl (the seated variation)

**Being Comfortable at the Computer** - Water, Brain Buttons, Balance Buttons, Neck Rolls, Hook-ups

**Reading without Eyestrain** - Water, Brain Buttons, Earth Buttons, Lazy 8s, The Cross Crawl, Think of an X

**Speed-Reading** - The Calf Pump, The Cross Crawl, Lazy 8s, Think of an X

**Organizing Paperwork** - The Double Doodle, The Rocker, Positive Points

**Paying Attention to Detail** - Brain Buttons, The Cross Crawl, Earth Buttons, Lazy 8s

**Setting Priorities** - Space Buttons, The Thinking Cap, The Cross Crawl, Hook-ups

**Maintaining Confidence** - Balance Buttons, Earth Buttons, Space Buttons

**Handling Criticism** - The Calf Pump, Hook-ups, Positive Points

**Keeping a Sense of Humor** - The Rocker, Arm Activation, The Thinking Cap, The Energy Yawn, Hook-ups

**Maintaining Postural Flexibility** - Arm Activation, The Cross Crawl, The Gravity Glider, The Energizer

**Following Through** - Hook-ups, The Energy Yawn, The Footflex, The Calf Pump

# Task Index

To use the following index of work skills, scan the alphabetized key words (those in bold type) to determine which skills you want to address and which menu of Brain Gym activities can be used to enhance those skills. Each menu offers a suggested sequence of movements, developed through years of empirical research. Over time, you may discover your own preferred order for doing the Brain Gym activities.

Comfortable **AIR TRAVEL** - Balance Buttons, The Elephant, Lazy 8s,
 The Cross Crawl, Hook-ups, Positive Points

Comfort Working **ALONE** - Water, Brain Buttons, The Cross Crawl, Hook-ups

Appreciating Your Own **APPEARANCE** - Earth Buttons, Space Buttons,
 Balance Buttons

Being **ASSERTIVE** - Balance Buttons, Hook-ups, Positive Points

Operating **ATM MACHINES** - Water, Brain Buttons, Earth Buttons, Space Buttons,
 Lazy 8s

Organizing **BULK MAILINGS** - Water, The Grounder, The Cross Crawl,
 Think of an X

**COLD CALLING** - Positive Points, The Thinking Cap, The Owl, The Cross Crawl

Working in **COLUMNS** - Brain Buttons, The Cross Crawl, Earth Buttons,
 Space Buttons, Lazy 8s

**COMMUNICATING** Effectively - The Calf Pump, The Footflex, Lazy 8s,
 The Energy Yawn

**COMMUNICATING** with Clients - The Energy Yawn, The Footflex,
 The Calf Pump, The Gravity Glider

Handling **COMPLAINTS** - The Footflex, The Gravity Glider, The Calf Pump

**COMPOSING** Letters - The Calf Pump, The Footflex, The Owl, The Energy Yawn

Being Comfortable at the **COMPUTER** - Water, Brain Buttons, Balance Buttons,
 Neck Rolls, Hook-ups

Maintaining **CONFIDENCE** - Balance Buttons, Earth Buttons, Space Buttons

Projecting **CONFIDENCE** - The Thinking Cap, The Owl, The Cross Crawl,
 Positive Points

Giving **CONSTRUCTIVE CRITICISM** - Neck Rolls, The Energy Yawn,
 Belly Breathing

Modeling Good **CO-WORKER RELATIONS** - The Cross Crawl, The Rocker,
 Neck Rolls, The Energy Yawn, Belly Breathing

Accessing **CREATIVITY** - The Double Doodle, The Footflex, The Calf Pump,
 The Energy Yawn

Handling **CRITICISM** - The Calf Pump, Hook-ups, Positive Points

Entering **DATA** with Speed, Accuracy, and Comfort - Water, Brain Buttons,
 Neck Rolls, Hook-ups

Paying Attention to **DETAIL** - Brain Buttons, The Cross Crawl, Earth Buttons,
Lazy 8s

**DICTATING** into a Computer - Water, The Thinking Cap, Hook-ups

Dealing with **DISAPPOINTMENT** - Positive Points, Hook-ups

**DRIVING** with Comfort - Balance Buttons, Lazy 8s, Hook-ups, Positive Points

Maintaining **ENTHUSIASM** - Hook-ups, The Calf Pump, The Gravity Glider

Troubleshooting of **EQUIPMENT** Problems - Earth Buttons, Space Buttons, The Energizer, Hook-ups

Organizing and Completing **ERRANDS** - The Thinking Cap, Lazy 8s, The Cross Crawl

Preventing **EYESTRAIN** at the Computer - Water, Brain Buttons, The Cross Crawl, Lazy 8s

Reading without **EYESTRAIN** - Water, Brain Buttons, Earth Buttons, Lazy 8s, The Cross Crawl, Think of an X

**FILING** - Balance Buttons, Earth Buttons, Space Buttons

Maintaining Postural **FLEXIBILITY** - Arm Activation, The Cross Crawl, The Gravity Glider, The Energizer

**FOCUSING** Attention - The Calf Pump, The Footflex, The Gravity Glider, The Owl

**FOLLOWING THROUGH** - Hook-ups, The Energy Yawn, The Footflex, The Calf Pump

**FOLLOWING UP** - The Rocker, The Energizer, The Cross Crawl

Filling Out **FORMS** - Arm Activation, The Double Doodle, Alphabet 8s, The Energy Yawn

Setting and Meeting **GOALS** - Water, Brain Buttons, The Cross Crawl, Hook-ups

**HANDLING OBJECTIONS** Calmly - The Energy Yawn, Neck Rolls, Belly Breathing

Keeping a Sense of **HUMOR** - The Rocker, Arm Activation, The Thinking Cap, The Energy Yawn, Hook-ups

**INPUTTING** with Accuracy - Brain Buttons, Balance Buttons, Earth Buttons, The Thinking Cap

Carrying Out **INSTRUCTIONS** - The Thinking Cap, Balance Buttons, The Owl, The Elephant, The Cross Crawl, Hook-ups

Conducting **INTERVIEWS** - The Footflex, The Calf Pump, The Energy Yawn, Lazy 8s

Maintaining **INVENTORY AND SUPPLIES** - The Cross Crawl, The Grounder, The Gravity Glider, The Owl, The Energizer

Coordinating **INVOICES AND PRODUCTS** - Balance Buttons, The Owl,
The Cross Crawl, Lazy 8s

Coordinating Processes at the **KEYBOARD** - Arm Activation, The Double Doodle,
Lazy 8s, Alphabet 8s

**KEYBOARDING** with Dexterity - Brain Buttons, Balance Buttons, Earth Buttons,
Arm Activation, The Double Doodle, Lazy 8s

Expressing **LEADERSHIP SKILLS** - The Footflex, The Calf Pump, Lazy 8s,
The Energy Yawn

Leaving **VOICE MAIL MESSAGES** - Hook-ups, The Energy Yawn,
The Calf Pump, The Energizer

Interpreting **LEGAL CODES AND LANGUAGE** - Brain Buttons, Earth Buttons,
Lazy 8s, Positive Points

**LISTENING** Actively and Attentively - The Thinking Cap, The Elephant, The Owl

Working with **LISTS** on the Computer - Earth Buttons, Space Buttons,
Balance Buttons

Using **MATH** Skills - Earth Buttons, Space Buttons, Balance Buttons,
The Thinking Cap, The Owl, The Energy Yawn

Using **MECHANICAL SKILLS** - Brain Buttons, Arm Activation, The Cross Crawl

Leading **MEETINGS** - The Calf Pump, Brain Buttons, Balance Buttons, Hook-ups

**MEMORIZING** a Script - The Owl, The Elephant, The Energy Yawn,
The Thinking Cap

Accessing **MEMORY** - The Elephant, The Owl, The Thinking Cap

Handling **MULTIPLE TASKS** - Brain Buttons, The Grounder, Hook-ups

Holding to **OBJECTIVES** - Balance Buttons, Hook-ups, Positive Points

**PACKING** and Categorizing Boxes - The Grounder, The Gravity Glider,
Brain Buttons, Earth Buttons, Space Buttons

Filling Out Repetitive **PAPERWORK** - Brain Buttons, Earth Buttons,
Arm Activation, Lazy 8s, Alphabet 8s

Organizing **PAPERWORK** - The Double Doodle, The Rocker, Positive Points

Maintaining Comfort with **PEOPLE** - The Calf Pump, The Footflex,
The Energy Yawn, The Energizer

Handling **PERSONNEL DECISIONS** - The Footflex, The Grounder,
The Calf Pump, The Gravity Glider

**PLANNING** Long-Range Strategies - The Calf Pump, The Grounder,
The Gravity Glider, The Elephant

Seeing Other **POINTS OF VIEW** - The Calf Pump, The Footflex, Hook-ups

Maintaining **POSITIVE ENERGY** - Positive Points, Hook-ups, Balance Buttons

Setting **PRIORITIES** - Space Buttons, The Thinking Cap, The Cross Crawl,
Hook-ups

**PROBLEM SOLVING** - The Cross Crawl, Balance Buttons, Neck Rolls,
Positive Points

Remembering **PRODUCT KNOWLEDGE** - Balance Buttons, Neck Rolls,
The Cross Crawl, Positive Points

Maximizing **PROGRAMMING** Abilities - The Calf Pump, The Elephant,
Neck Rolls, The Owl

**PUBLIC SPEAKING** - The Elephant, The Owl, The Energy Yawn,
The Thinking Cap, The Cross Crawl, Hook-ups,
Positive Points

Answering **QUESTIONS** - The Calf Pump, The Grounder, The Footflex

Meeting **QUOTAS** - Earth Buttons, Space Buttons, Balance Buttons

Developing **RAPPORT** - The Footflex, The Energy Yawn, Lazy 8s, The Calf Pump

Speed-**READING** - The Calf Pump, The Cross Crawl, Lazy 8s, Think of an X

**READING** Aloud - The Rocker, Neck Rolls, The Energy Yawn, Belly Breathing

**READING** with Accuracy - Water, Brain Buttons, Earth Buttons, Lazy 8s,
The Cross Crawl

**READING** with Comprehension - The Footflex, The Gravity Glider, The Grounder,
The Calf Pump

Handling **REJECTION** - Belly Breathing, Neck Rolls, The Energy Yawn,
Positive Points, Hook-ups

Managing **RESOURCES** - Balance Buttons, Earth Buttons, Space Buttons

Delegating **RESPONSIBILITY** - The Grounder, The Gravity Glider, The Owl

Taking **RESPONSIBILITY** - Positive Points, Think of an X, Belly Breathing

Staying on **SCHEDULE** - Belly Breathing, Earth Buttons, Balance Buttons,
Positive Points, Hook-ups

Accessing Positive **SELF-CONCEPT** - Positive Points, Hook-ups, Balance Buttons

Maintaining **SELF-CONTROL** - Balance Buttons, Hook-ups, Positive Points

**SEQUENCING** Numbers with Precision - The Calf Pump, The Elephant, Neck Rolls, The Owl, The Gravity Glider, The Double Doodle

**SETTING LIMITS** - Positive Points, Hook-ups, Balance Buttons

**SITTING** Comfortably - Arm Activation, The Grounder, The Gravity Glider, The Cross Crawl (the seated variation)

Solving **SOFTWARE** Problems - Earth Buttons, Space Buttons, The Energizer, Hook-ups

**SPEAKING** Clearly - The Energy Yawn, The Thinking Cap, The Elephant, Hook-ups

**SPELLING** with Accuracy - Earth Buttons, The Elephant, The Thinking Cap, The Owl

**STAYING CALM** - Earth Buttons, Hook-ups, Positive Points

Using **TACT** - The Calf Pump, The Grounder, The Gravity Glider, The Footflex

Working as Part of a **TEAM** - The Double Doodle, The Footflex, The Calf Pump

**TEAM-BUILDING** - The Rocker, The Calf Pump, Balance Buttons, The Cross Crawl, Lazy 8s

Maintaining **TELEPHONE VOICE QUALITY** - The Elephant, The Energy Yawn, The Owl, The Thinking Cap, Hook-ups

Feeling Comfortable on the **TELEPHONE** - Balance Buttons, The Elephant, The Owl, Arm Activation, The Energy Yawn, The Thinking Cap

Answering **TELEPHONES** - The Thinking Cap, The Elephant, The Owl

Holding to **VALUES** - The Calf Pump, The Footflex, The Energy Yawn, Hook-ups

Maintaining **VERSATILITY** - The Footflex, The Rocker, The Cross Crawl (the seated variation), The Energizer

**WRITING** Legibly - Arm Activation, The Double Doodle, Lazy 8s, Alphabet 8s

Effective **WRITING** - The Calf Pump, The Footflex, The Owl, The Energy Yawn

# Brain Gym Activities

As you do the movements detailed in these pages—in fact, as you carry out all your daily activities—we suggest that you keep in mind the following:

## The Key to Coordinated Breathing

Whether you bend, lengthen, or lift . . .
*ex*hale on movements where you are *ex*tending or *ex*erting yourself,
and *in*hale when drawing your limbs or your energy back *in*.

That's all you need to remember for balanced coordination of movement and breathing. This will become more automatic the longer you practice the Brain Gym system.

# ALPHABET 8s

Center a piece of paper or other writing surface directly in front of you. With a pen or pencil, begin drawing continuous and overlapping figure 8s lying on their sides (See figure 1, page 31).

Step 1: Draw three 8s with your left hand, then three with your right hand, then three using both hands together. Keep your eyes focused on the pen or pencil point (See figure 1).

Step 2: Draw three 8s with your writing hand. Without stopping, draw a lowercase printed-style "a" on top of the left-hand side of the last 8. Continue with two more 8s (See figure 2).

Step 3: Draw three more 8s. Starting with a downward stroke on the central line, draw a "b" on the right-hand side of the last 8. Continue with two more 8s (See figure 2).

Step 4: Repeat the same sequence, using a letter "c" on the left half, and then a sequence ending with a "d" on the left (See figure 3).

## What Alphabet 8s Do

Alphabet 8s, an adaptation of Lazy 8s, integrate the movement involved in the formation of printed letters. For many people, experiencing the similarities of the letters, rather than just their distinctions, enables them to write more automatically, freeing the mind for creative thought.

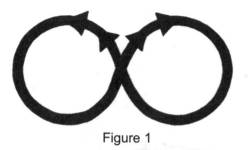

Figure 1

Figure 2

Figure 3

# ARM ACTIVATION

**R**each with your right arm straight up toward the ceiling. Place your left hand above your right shoulder on the arm muscle. Slowly and gently exhale through your mouth while pressing your right arm isometrically against your left hand for about eight seconds in a forward direction. Inhale as you relax your pressure. Continue this process by exhaling as you move your left hand to press in all three other directions: toward your ear, away from it, and to the rear. Repeat the entire sequence for the other arm.

## What Arm Activation Does

Arm Activation lengthens the muscles of the upper chest and shoulders, where muscular control for both gross- and fine-motor activities originates. This movement relaxes and coordinates shoulder and arm muscles and frees the mind for ease of handwriting, spelling, and creative writing.

# BALANCE BUTTONS

Place two or more fingertips behind one ear, about three finger widths away from the ear. Put your other hand on your navel, and hold for 30 seconds to one minute as you breathe deeply. If you experience tension behind your ear, make small circles with your nose, thus pressing your head against your fingers and massaging the area. Change hands and repeat on the other side.

## What Balance Buttons Do

Balance Buttons stimulate the body's balance system in the inner ear. This restores your sense of equilibrium, relaxing your eyes and the rest of your body and freeing your attention for easier thought and action. Decision making, concentration, and problem solving all improve as body organization improves.

# BELLY BREATHING

Place your hands on your abdomen. Exhale through your mouth in short little puffs, as if you are keeping a feather in the air, until your lungs feel empty.

Now inhale deeply, filling yourself like a balloon beneath your hand. (By arching your back slightly, you can take in even more air.) Then slowly and fully exhale. Repeat this inhalation and exhalation, establishing a natural rhythm, during the course of three or more breaths.

## What Belly Breathing Does

Belly Breathing improves the supply of oxygen to the entire body, especially the brain, via the blood. It relaxes the central nervous system while increasing your energy level. Diaphragmatic breathing has been found to improve both reading and speaking abilities.

# BRAIN BUTTONS

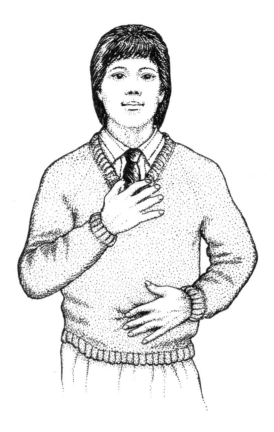

Rest one hand over your navel. With the thumb and fingers of the other hand, feel for the two hollow areas under the collarbone about one inch out from the center of the chest, where the collarbone meets the sternum. Rub these areas vigorously for 30 seconds to one minute, as you look left to right and right to left.

## What Brain Buttons Do

Brain Buttons stimulate the carotid arteries that supply freshly oxygenated blood to the brain. They help reestablish directional messages from parts of the body to the brain and the visual system, thus improving the brain's "cross-talk" for reading, writing, speaking, or following directions.

# THE CALF PUMP

Stand arm's length away from a wall and place your hands (shoulder-width apart) against it. Extend your left leg straight out behind you, so that the ball of your foot is on the floor and your heel is off the floor. Your body is slanted at a 45 degree angle.

Exhale, leaning forward against the wall while also bending your right knee and pressing your left heel against the floor. The more you bend the front knee, the more lengthening you will feel in the back of the left calf. Inhale and raise yourself back up, while relaxing and raising the left heel. Do the movement three or more times, completing a breath with each cycle. Then alternate to the other leg and repeat.

## What the Calf Pump Does

The Calf Pump restores a more natural length to the muscles and tendons in the back of the body. This releases the reflex to hold back and the associated feelings of being unable to participate in activities or to take positive action. Doing the Calf Pump improves concentration, attention, comprehension, and the ability to bring projects to closure.

# THE CROSS CRAWL

Standing, "march" in place, alternately touching each hand to the opposite knee. Continue during the course of four to eight complete, relaxed breaths. A variation of this movement can be done sitting down.

## What the Cross Crawl Does

Cross Crawl activates both brain hemispheres simultaneously. It engages the brain for coordinating visual, auditory, and kinesthetic abilities, thus improving such skills as listening, reading, writing, and memory.

# THE DOUBLE DOODLE

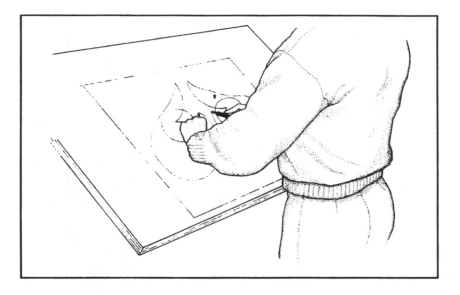

Hold a pen or other writing implement in each hand. On a large sheet of paper, draw mirrored shapes using both hands simultaneously, allowing one hand to lead while the other follows. Begin by drawing large, simple shapes, like circles, squares, or triangles. At first, it may be helpful to be aware of "up," "down," "in," and "out" as you move. As this feels comfortable, you can graduate to more creative and playful designs.

## What the Double Doodle Does

Double Doodle is a bilateral drawing activity that will establish directionality and orientation in space, relative to the midline of the body. It exercises eye-teaming abilities and assists in developing hand-eye coordination for improved writing skills.

# EARTH BUTTONS

Rest two fingers of one hand under your lower lip. Place the heel of the other hand on your navel, with fingers pointing downward. Breathe deeply as you look at the floor. Moving only your eyes, look gradually from the floor to the ceiling, then down again. Repeat this for three or more breaths, as your eyes and entire body relax.

## What Earth Buttons Do

Earth Buttons are located on the body's front midline, the central point of reference across which all tasks involving both sides of the body must be coordinated. Holding these points stimulates the brain and relieves mental fatigue, as well as increasing organizational skills and enhancing the ability to focus on near objects.

# THE ELEPHANT

Stand with your feet about shoulder-width apart. Face a wall across the room, and on it picture a large figure 8 on its side. Bend your knees and extend your left arm out in front of you. Tilt your head, touching your left ear to your left shoulder.

Lifting from the waist, point the index finger of your extended arm and begin to trace the 8 by moving your hand up the center of your body and to the left. Breathe deeply as you focus your eyes past your hand (ideally, you will see a double image of your hand). Continue to trace three or more 8s, then repeat with the right arm extended and the right ear touching your right shoulder.

## What the Elephant Does

Neck-muscle tension is often caused by a chronic avoidance of turning the head to listen. The Elephant releases muscle tension in the neck which may have inhibited the perception of sound, restoring natural flexibility to the neck. It integrates the left and right sides of the brain for increased listening comprehension, short- and long-term memory, and abstract thinking.

# THE ENERGIZER

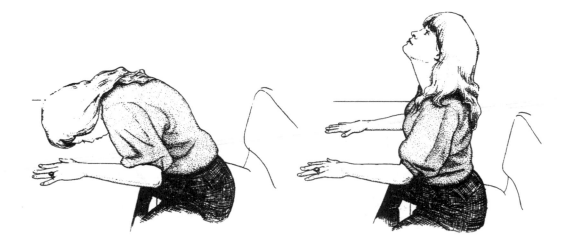

Sit on a chair in front of a table, resting your forehead between your hands on the table top. Exhale fully. Now, while slowly lifting your head, inhale deeply, breathing into the base of your spine. Your torso and shoulders should stay relaxed. As you exhale, tuck your chin down onto your chest and begin moving your head down toward the table while lengthening the back of your neck. Rest your head on the table as you relax and breathe deeply. Repeat three or more times.

## What the Energizer Does

This movement keeps the back muscles toned and the spine supple, flexible, and relaxed. Doing the activity improves posture, concentration, and attention, and is especially useful while working at a desk or computer.

# THE ENERGY YAWN

As you begin to yawn, lightly press the finger-tips of each hand against any tight spots you feel where your cheeks cover your upper and lower molars. Make a deep, relaxed, yawning sound while gently stroking away any tension. Repeat the Energy Yawn three or more times.

## What the Energy Yawn Does

More than 50 percent of the neurological connections from the brain to the rest of the body pass through the jaw joints. Massaging the area over the muscles that open and close the mouth relaxes the jaw, freeing these connections for increased whole-brain integration.

The Energy Yawn also relaxes the eyes by stimulating lubrication. For many people, there is a positive relationship between ease of jaw motion, ease of expression, and even creative ability.

# THE FOOTFLEX

**S**itting, rest your right ankle on your left knee. Place one hand behind your right knee, on the end of the calf muscle. The other hand holds the Achilles tendon, right behind the ankle bone. Point and flex the right foot five or more times while holding your hands firmly at both positions. Feel the muscle lengthening and relaxing. Now place both feet on the floor and notice how different the two legs feel before repeating the movement with your left ankle on your right knee. Some people experience even greater benefits by straightening the leg as they hold the points and do the flexion.

## What the Footflex Does
The Footflex restores the natural length of the tendons in the calf area. It relaxes the reflex to hold back, while increasing the abilities to communicate, to concentrate, and to complete tasks.

# THE GRAVITY GLIDER

Sit comfortably in a chair. Cross your ankles and bend your knees slightly. Exhale slowly as you lean forward with your head down, reaching out in front of you and letting your arms glide out parallel to your legs. Reach as far as you comfortably can. Now inhale as you glide back upright, bringing your head up last. Continue during the course of three or more complete breaths. Then cross your ankles the other way and repeat the process.

## What the Gravity Glider Does

When the muscles in the hips (the ileopsoas muscle group) tighten in response to sitting for long periods or to stress in the pelvic area, movement, flexibility, and even circulation of blood and lymph are restricted. Relaxation of this muscle group is essential for balance and whole-body coordination, and contributes to comprehension. The Gravity Glider lengthens and relaxes these muscles.

# THE GROUNDER

Stand with your legs a little less than one leg-length apart. Point your left foot toward the left. Keep your hips tucked under, with your body facing squarely forward. Now bend your left knee as you exhale, keeping the right knee straight. As you inhale, straighten the bent knee and draw yourself upright again. Do the movement over the course of three or more complete breaths, then repeat it while facing in the other direction. As a variation, place the foot of the bending leg on a chair seat as you do the movement. In either case, the knee is protected by being extended no further than the middle of the foot.

## What the Grounder Does

The Grounder lengthens and relaxes the ileopsoas muscle group in the hips, which balances and stabilizes the body. Doing the movement increases comprehension, short-term memory, self-expression, and organizational skills.

# HOOK-UPS

## PART ONE

Stand with your feet flat on the floor. Cross your left ankle over your right ankle. Next, extend your arms with the backs of your hands facing each other and cross the left wrist over the right so that your palms touch. Interlace your fingers and swing your hands down and then up onto your chest. On inhalation, place your tongue flat against the roof of your mouth, approximately one quarter inch behind your front teeth; lower it on exhalation. Repeat the tongue placements, relaxing in this position during the course of four to eight complete breaths.

## PART TWO

Uncross your legs, placing your feet flat on the floor. Lightly join the fingertips of both hands together, as though enclosing a ball. Close your eyes as you continue to lift your tongue on inhalation and lower it on exhalation, relaxing in this position during the course of four to eight complete breaths.

## What Hook-ups Do

The Hook-ups movement was first developed by Wayne Cook, a researcher on electromagnetic energy. Paul and Gail Dennison developed the variation presented here. Part One simultaneously connects all the energy circuits in the body and stimulates the movement of any blocked energy. Touching the fingertips in Part Two balances and connects the two hemispheres of the brain. This strengthens the body's electromagnetic energy, especially in environments that contain strong electric fields from computers, fluorescent lights, television, or air conditioning. Reported benefits are increased vitality, an improved self-concept, and an enhanced sense of personal boundaries.

# LAZY 8s

Extend one arm straight out in front of you, with the thumb pointing toward the ceiling. In the air, slowly and smoothly trace the shape of a large figure 8 on its side. As you draw the 8, focus your eyes on your thumb. Keep your neck relaxed and head upright, letting your head move slightly with the motion of the 8.

Start tracing your Lazy 8 by beginning at eye level, directly in front of the center of your body. Move your arm up and over to the left, around and back to center, then to the right. Do three full 8s with one hand, then three with the other, and finally three with both hands clasped together.

## What Lazy 8s Do

Lazy 8s integrate the left and right visual fields, thus increasing left and right hemispheric integration while improving balance and coordination. Many people report better binocular vision and increased peripheral vision after doing the Lazy 8s. Reading, writing, and comprehension skills improve as the physical mechanics of these tasks become easier and the attention is freed for focused mental activity.

# NECK ROLLS

While breathing deeply, relax your shoulders and drop your head forward. Close your eyes while slowly and easily rolling your head from side to side. At any point of tension, relax your head while making small circles with your nose and breathing fully. Do three or more complete side-to-side motions.

## What Neck Rolls Do

Tension in the neck is often caused by a tightening of the muscles in the throat while verbalizing or thinking. Neck Rolls release these tense muscles, increasing the ability to do mental activities without stress. Doing Neck Rolls also improves breathing and increases relaxation of vocal cords for more resonant speech. As there is improvement in the ability to move the eyes left to right across the visual midfield, reading ability also improves.

# THE OWL

**W**ith your left hand, grasp the top of your right shoulder muscle, near the neck, and squeeze it firmly. Inhale deeply. Exhale as you turn your head to look comfortably back over your right shoulder; inhale as you return your head to the center. Exhale as you turn your head to look back over your left shoulder; inhale as you return your head to the center. Now exhale as you drop your head forward, lowering your chin to your chest. Inhale as you raise your head again. Repeat over three or more breaths in each of the three directions, as your shoulder and neck relax. Now do the Owl movement while squeezing the left shoulder with the right hand, repeating over three or more breaths in each direction.

## What the Owl Does

The Owl releases tension in the muscles of the shoulders and neck, thus restoring range of motion for turning the head. Neck-muscle tension is commonly caused by chronic subvocalization when reading, or by resisting the natural impulse to turn the head to listen. As the neck muscles relax, listening comprehension (as well as thinking and speaking abilities) improves.

# POSITIVE POINTS

The Positive Points are located above the center of each eyebrow and halfway to the hairline. You might find a slight bulge at each point. Lightly place three fingers of each hand on these points. (Some people, when holding their own points, will prefer to cross their hands so that the right hand goes to the left side of the forehead.) Close your eyes and hold the points lightly during the course of six to ten slow, complete breaths.

You can hold your own Positive Points or have a partner hold them for you. To further release stress, hold the points while reviewing the stress-producing situation and considering alternative possibilities.

## What Positive Points Do

The Positive Points are acupressure points specifically known for diffusing the fight-or-flight reflex, thus releasing emotional stress. Touching these points transfers the brain response to stress from the midbrain to the front part of the brain (the frontal lobe), allowing a more rational response.

# THE ROCKER

Sit on a padded surface on the floor with your knees bent and your feet together in front of you. Lean back, with your weight on your hands and hips. Rock yourself in small circles, or back and forth, as you focus on melting away any areas of tension in your hips or in the backs of your legs.

## What the Rocker Does

In this movement, massage of the hamstrings and hips helps to release tense muscles in the back of the body that keep you from moving forward with ease. The Rocker increases the flow of cerebrospinal fluid to the brain, thus improving the ability to focus, concentrate, and comprehend. When the hips and lower back are relaxed, sitting is also more centered and comfortable.

# SPACE BUTTONS

Rest two fingers above your upper lip. Place your other hand, pointing downward, on your lower back, with your fingertips touching the tailbone. Breathe deeply as you look up at the ceiling. Gradually lower your gaze to the floor, then look up at the ceiling again. Repeat three or more times as your eyes and the rest of your body relax.

## What Space Buttons Do
The Space Buttons are located near the top and bottom of the central nervous system, which includes the spinal column, hindbrain, midbrain (behind the eyes and nose), and cerebral cortex. Holding the two points stimulates movement throughout the system, which improves attention, focus, motivation, and intuition for decision making.

# THINK OF AN X

Look at the X on this page for a few moments, or close your eyes and visualize the letter X. Notice how your vision is like the X–your eyes coordinate to connect left, right, upper, and lower visual fields around a point of focus. Also notice the X-like symmetry and organization within your own body, as each hip coordinates with its opposite shoulder.

## What Think of an X Does
The X represents the ability to cross the midline that connects right and left visual fields, right and left sides of the body for movement, and both hemispheres of the brain for integrated thought processes. The X is a reminder to use both eyes and both sides of the body. It reinforces whole-brain and whole-body coordination for ease of thought, communication, and performance of all kinds.

# THE THINKING CAP

With one hand at the top of each ear, gently "unroll" the curved parts at the outer edges of both ears at the same time. Continue all the way to the bottom of the ears. Repeat three or more times.

## What the Thinking Cap Does

Doing the Thinking Cap helps you to tune out distracting noises and to tune into meaningful rhythms and sounds, such as those of music or spoken language. This movement increases listening ability, short-term memory, and abstract thinking skills.

# An Overview of Experimental Research Using Brain Gym

The following is a compilation of professional publications and research abstracts from presentations at various conferences. It deals with the experimental research that has been completed using Brain Gym and other Educational Kinesiology techniques in controlled situations. Each reference is followed by a summary of the information contained within the longer work.

## Publications

Khalsa, Guruchiter Kaur, Morris, G.S. Don, & Sifft, Josie M. (1988). Effect of Educational Kinesiology on the static balance of learning-disabled students. *Perceptual and Motor Skills*, 67, 51-54.

> This publication is the short research journal report of the first experimental study conducted using Educational Kinesiology techniques. The study was conducted by Guruchiter Kaur Khalsa as a Master's thesis in the Department of Health, Physical Education, and Recreation at the California State Polytechnic University.

Khalsa, Guruchiter K. and Sifft, Josie M. (1988). The effects of Educational Kinesiology upon the static balance of learning disabled boys and girls. (ERIC Document Reproduction Service No. ED 289 835)

> This publication, the hard copy of a presentation made to the American Alliance for Health, Physical Education, Recreation and Dance National Convention in Las Vegas, Nevada, in April of 1987, provides detailed information on the first experimental study conducted using Educational Kinesiology techniques, including some Brain Gym activities and Dennison Laterality Repatterning. The full publication is available from Educational Resources Information Center, or can be viewed on microfiche.

Sifft Josie M. (1990). Educational Kinesiology: Empowering students and athletes through movement. (ERIC Document Reproduction Service No. ED 320891)

> This publication, the hard copy of a presentation made to the American Alliance for Health, Physical Education, Recreation and Dance National Convention in New Orleans, Louisiana, in April of 1990, provides an overview of Educational Kinesiology, an explanation of some of the Brain Gym activities, and a report of the research to date. The full publication is available from Educational Resources Information Center, or can be viewed on microfiche.

Sifft, Josie M., and G.C.K. Khalsa (1991). Effect of Educational Kinesiology upon simple response times and choice response times. *Perceptual and Motor Skills,* 73, 1011-1015.

> This publication is the short research journal report of the second experimental study conducted using Educational Kinesiology techniques. The study was done with university students to see whether Brain Gym activities and Laterality Repatterning would influence the response times to a visual stimulus. The results indicated that both Edu-K groups were superior to the control group and that the Repatterned group improved twice as much as the Brain Gym-only group.

# Selected Research Abstracts

"Effect of Educational Kinesiology upon the Static Balance of Learning-Disabled Boys and Girls," G.C.K. Khalsa and Josie M. Sifft, Ph.D., American Alliance for Health, Physical Education, Recreation and Dance National Convention, April, 1987, Las Vegas, Nevada.

> This study was completed with 60 learning-disabled elementary students. An equal number of boys and girls were divided into three groups: Repatterned Edu-K, Edu-K movement, and a control. The results indicated that the Repatterned Edu-K group showed a greater improvement in static balance than the Edu-K movement group, who in turn performed better than the control group. The findings also suggest that Edu-K can be used effectively in a coeducational setting.

"Effect of Educational Kinesiology Upon Simple and Four-Choice Response Times." Josie M. Sifft, Ph.D. and G.C.K. Khalsa. American Alliance for Health, Physical Education, Recreation and Dance Southwest District Convention, March, 1989, Salt Lake City, Utah.

> This study completed with university students compares a control group with two experimental groups, one using only Brain Gym activities, and the other experiencing Dennison Laterality Repatterning and the Brain Gym activities. The results indicated that the EduK groups were superior to the control group in their response time to a four-choice visual light display. The repatterned group improved by twice the amount of the Brain Gym-only group.

"Effect of Educational Kinesiology on Hearing." Josie M. Sifft, Ph.D. and G.C.K. Khalsa. California Association for Health, Physical Education, Recreation and Dance Regional Conference, December, 1990, Long Beach, California.

> This study was completed with 16 elementary school teachers who served as their own control. Each teacher was tested on the Pure-tone audiometer before and after one of two types of movement experiences. The movement experience was either 10 minutes of random movements about the room or a series of five Brain Gym activities. The results indicated that after the Brain Gym activities the hearing of the teachers who did these activities was better than those who did the random movements.

"Effect of Educational Kinesiology on Response Times of Learning-Disabled Students." G.C.K. Khalsa and Josie M. Sifft, Ph.D.

> This study was completed in 1988 with 52 children selected from Special Education classes. A Brain Gym group performed a sequence of activities, while a control group engaged in random movements for about seven minutes. All children were tested for visual response time before and after the movement activities. The results indicated that those children exposed to the Brain Gym movements improved on the response-time task, while those in the control group did not.

# Related Experimental and Field Study Summaries

"Brain Gym® and Its Effect on Reading Abilities." Cecilia K. Freeman, M.ED., © 2000.
This study was completed using a non-equivalent control group design. 205 students were assigned to either the Brain Gym or control group. Throughout the school year, 12 teachers incorporated Brain Gym in the classroom curricula so that the students and teachers did a minimum of 15 minutes of Brain Gym per day. Equal samples of students were randomly selected for the Brain Gym group and the control group who did not use brain Gym, and their test scores were compared. The results indicated that those children in the Brain Gym group improved their reading abilities, as measured by a standardized test, twice as much as those in the control group.

"The Effect of PACE on Self-Related Anxiety and Performance in First-Year Nursing Students." Jan Irving, R.N., Ph.D., © 1995.
This multiple baseline design was completed with 27 first-year nursing students, using three separate groups as controls during the different phases of the nine-week study. The study measured the effects of four Brain Gym activities making up a six-minute sequence known as the PACE process, on weekly assessments of self-reported anxiety and performance on fourteen technical-motor skill tests. The PACE group experienced a 69.5 percent reduction in self-reported anxiety and an 18.7 percent increase in performance on skill tests as compared to continued self-reporting of high anxiety and higher failure rate in the control groups not using PACE.

"Effects of Edu-K on Computer-Related Eye-and-Muscle Strain of Adults." Joan Spalding, M.S., © 1990.
In 1990, Joan Spalding, M.S., of Mancato State University, conducted this one group pre-test/post-test pilot study in partial fulfillment of the requirements towards her Master's Degree. The purpose of the study was to determine whether Edu-K Brain Gym® and Vision Gym™ activities have an effect on eye and muscle strain or other physical symptoms generated by use of a computer video display terminal (VDT). The project was conducted over a six week period. Ten subjects from twenty-nine to fifty years who used the VDT as a principal part of their work (four or more hours daily) punctuated each hour of computer time with a five-minute break for Edu-K movements. Half the subjects were male; half female. Half were entrepreneurs, half salaried employees. Satistically statistically results indicated that computer breaks for Edu-K activities contributed to a lessening of visual and muscle-related stress but had no measurable effect on other physical symptoms.

"The Results of Preliminary and Follow-up Questionnaires Administered to Salespersons Attending Switched-On Selling Seminars." Jerry V. Teplitz, J.D., Ph.D.

This study, completed in 1992 analyzed the attitudinal changes of participants who attended a one-day Switched-On Selling seminar toward various elements of the sales process. Participants completed a questionnaire at the beginning of the class and again at the end of the session. The seminar did not teach technique; rather, it covered all aspects of the selling process, such as prospecting, presenting and follow-up, and used preselected Brain Gym® activities. Eighteen questions were asked of each of the 149 participants. The two questions that revealed the highest level of change were "I handle rejection well" and "It is easy for me to make cold calls using the telephone." On the question "I handle rejection well," the number of salespersons in disagreement with this at the beginning of the seminar dropped from 56% to only 8% at the conclusion of the seminar. On the question "It is easy for me to make cold calls using the telephone," on the prequestionnaire only 42% agreed or strongly agreed with this question. At the end of the seminar, 90% responded "agree" or "strongly agree." The results indicated that Switched-On Selling could have a very positive impact on the attitudes of salespeople. What felt difficult at the beginning of the day felt easier to do at the end of the seminar.

"Impact of Brain Gym Processes on Sales of Insurance." Robert Donovan.

In 1993, The South Carolina Farm Bureau Insurance Company held an open enrollment for the Switched-On Selling (SOS) seminar, and about one-third of the sales force elected to participate. Participants in the one-day course learned the Brain Gym® movements, experienced Dennison Laterality Repatterning, and explored the applications of these processes to specific aspects of the selling process. For 120 days following the seminar, the company tracked results for the SOS group as well as those salespeople who did not attend the seminar. The results suggest that the SOS salespeople made a significant change in their performance. The SOS group increased the number of applications received for insurance policies by 39 percent, as compared to no increase for the control group. Similarly, the premiums earned by the SOS group went up to 101 percent, as compared to only a 30 percent increase for the non-SOS group.

# Bibliography and Recommended Reading

Anderson, Bob. *Stretching*. Bolinas, Calif.: Shelter Publications, Inc., 1980.

Buzan, Tony. *Use Both Sides of Your Brain*. New York: E.P. Dutton, 1976.

Carrigan, Catherine. *Healing Depression: A Guide to Making Intelligent Choices About Treating Depression*. New York: Heartsfire Books, 1997.

Childre, Doc, and Howard Martin with Donna Beech. *The Heartmath Solution*. NewYork: Harper Collins, 1999.

Churchland, Patricia Smith. *Neurophilosophy: Toward a Unified Science of the Mind/Brain*. Cambridge: The MTI Press, 1998.

Covey, Stephen R. *The 7 Habits of Highly Effective People*. New York: Simon & Schuster, Inc., 1990.

Csikszentmihalyi, Mihaly. *Flow: The Psychology of Optimal Experience*. New York: Harper Perennial, 1991.

Diamond, John, M.D. *BK: Behavioral Kinesiology*. New York: Archaeus Press, 1978.

Feldenkrais, Moshe. *Awareness through Movement: Health Exercises for Personal Growth*. San Francisco: Harper and Row, 1972.

Gardner, Howard, Ph.D. *Frames of Mind: The Theory of Multiple Intelligences*. New York: Basic Books, Inc., 1985.

Goodrich, Janet, Ph.D. *Natural Vision Improvement*. Berkeley: Celestial Arts, 1986.

Hannaford, Carla, Ph.D., *The Dominance Factor: How Knowing Your Dominant Eye, Ear, Brain, Hand, and Foot Can Improve Your Learning*. Arlington: Great Ocean Publishers, 1997.

Hannaford, Carla, Ph.D., *Smart Moves: Why Learning Is Not All in Your Head*. Arlington: Great Ocean Publishers, 1995.

Hanson, Dr. Peter. *The Joy of Stress*. London: Pan Books, Ltd., 1988.

Harmon, Darell Boyd. "Vision, Body Mechanics, and Performance." Optometric Extension Program: Santa Ana, Calif., 1958.

Hermann, Ned. *The Creative Brain*. Lake Hure, N.C.: Brain Books, 1988.

Kaplan, Robert-Michael. *The Power Behind Your Eyes: Improving Your Eyesight with Integrated Vision Therapy*. Rochester, Vermont: Healing Arts Press, 1995.

Leibowitz, Judith, and Bill Connington. *The Alexander Technique*. New York: Harper and Row, 1990.

Ornstein, Robert, and David Sobel. *The Healing Brain: Breakthrough Discoveries About How the Brain Keeps Us Healing*. New York: Simon and Schuster, 1987.

Ott, John. *Health and Light*. Old Greenwich, Conn.: The Devin-Adair Co., 1973.

Pearce, Joseph Chilton. *Evolution's End: Claiming the Potential of Our Intelligence*. New York: Harper Collins, 1992.

Promislow, Sharon. *Making the Brain-Body Connection*. West Vancouver, Canada: Kinetic Publishing Corporation, 1998.

Restak, Richard M., M.D. *The Brain: The Last Frontier*. New York: Warner Communications Co., 1980.

Robbins, Anthony. *Unlimited Power*. New York: Fawcett Columbine, 1986.

Rosenfield, Israel. *The Invention of Memory*. New York: Basic Books, Inc., 1988.

Springer, Sally, and Georg Deutsch. *Left Brain, Right Brain*. New York: W. H. Freeman and Co., 1989.

Thie, John F., D.C. *Touch for Health, rev. ed*. Marina del Rey, Calif.: DeVorss and Co., 1994.

## About the Authors

**Gail E. Dennison** has been a successful entrepreneur since the 1970s, when she operated her own day-care center in Southern California. She has 17 years of experience as an educator, including 10 years as a Touch for Health instructor, and is an internationally known speaker. She is the Vice President of the Edu-Kinesthetics, Inc., publishing company. She cofounded, and serves on the Board of Directors of, the nonprofit Educational Kinesiology Foundation, and is the founder and chief editor of the *Brain Gym Journal*. Gail is the coauthor and illustrator of the Brain Gym® books. She also created the Visioncircles course and Vision Gym movements for natural vision improvement.

**Paul E. Dennison, Ph.D.**, is an educator who has also found continued success in the business world. For nearly two decades, he owned and managed the Valley Remedial Group Learning Centers in California's San Fernando Valley. After 19 years in this enterprise, he had increased the number of these centers to eight. Since 1981, Dr. Dennison has owned his own publishing company, Edu-Kinesthetics, Inc., which has worldwide distribution. He is the author or coauthor of seven books and many manuals, all of which show the relationship of movement to high performance, and which include *Switching On: The Whole Brain Answer to Dyslexia*. He is Dean of Faculty of the Educational Kinesiology Foundation, the creator of the movement reeducation program called Brain Gym, a pioneer in applied brain research, and an international lecturer.

**Jerry V. Teplitz, J.D., Ph.D.**, is a graduate of Northwestern University School of Law, and practiced as an attorney for the Illinois Environmental Protection Agency. He holds both Masters and Doctorate degrees in Wholistic Health Sciences from Columbia Pacific University. The president of his own consulting firm for the last 32 years, Dr. Teplitz conducts keynotes and seminars in the areas of stress management, leadership, and sales development. He is a certified Brain Gym and Switched-On Golf Instructor, is the creator of the Switched-On Selling, Switched-On Management, and Switched-On Network Marketing Seminars, and has served on the Board of Directors of the Educational Kinesiology Foundation. Jerry is the author of *Managing Your Stress: How to Relax and Enjoy,* and a featured author in *Build a Better You–Starting Now* and *Switched-On Living*. He is listed in several editions of *Who's Who in America*.

# Edu-Kinesthetics Publications and Products

*All prices are in U.S. dollars.*

**Switching On** by Dr. Paul E. Dennison

*Switching On* presents easy-to-master techniques that you can use immediately to help students integrate left brain/right brain functions. The book introduces Educational Kinesiology, a unique merging of brain research, learning theory, and body awareness.

*Item #4306X    Switching On* ...............*$15.95*

**Edu-K for Kids** by Paul E. Dennison & Gail E. Dennison

*Edu-K for Kids* presents easy-to-understand visuals and step-by-step procedures that you can use immediately with children to integrate "try" and "reflex" brain functions. *Edu-K for Kids* is a book for parents and teachers to use with kids of all ages to facilitate Dennison Laterality Repatterning. Also available in Spanish as *Edu-K Para Chicos*.

*Item #43019    Edu-K for Kids* ...............*$15.95*

**Brain Gym®** and **Brain Gym® Teacher's Edition** by Paul E. Dennison and Gail E. Dennison

This companion to *Edu-K for Kids* is the book that reaches out to all with the message that movement and learning are necessary companions. Every page is full of high-energy illustrations of activities that are available to people of all ages. If you know that you or your child have the ability or the information but can't seem to "get it out," you need a copy of *Brain Gym*. *Teacher's Edition* also available.

*Item #43051    Brain Gym* ...............*$9.00*

*Item #43027    Brain Gym Teacher's Edition* ...............*$19.95*

**Personalized Whole Brain Integration** by Paul E. Dennison and Gail E. Dennison

This book will enable you to "switch on" to a higher level of brain performance and a deeper appreciation of your uniqueness, through an understanding of your brain-organization profile and how to maximize your innate potential through movement.

*Item #43078    Personalized Whole Brain Integration* ...............*$17.95*

**I Am the Child: Using Brain Gym With Children Who Have Special Needs**
by Cecilia K. Freeman with Gail E. Dennison

This book journals Freeman's experiences as a teacher in a public school where she offers a child-centered, cooperative model of learning. She shares her adaptations of the Brain Gym method as she successfully used it to meet the needs of eleven children with multiple challenges.

*Item #43108    I Am the Child* ...............*$17.95*

**The Learning Gym** by Erich Ballinger

Experience an introduction to the exciting Brain Gym program with this delightfully illustrated book that has captured the hearts of Europeans since its publication in 1992. A great gift for all ages.

*Item #43094    The Learning Gym* ...............*$14.95*

**Integrated Movements™** (audiotape) by Paul E. Dennison and Gail E. Dennison

The Integrated Movements, developed by Paul and Gail Dennison, balance body posture as well as twelve key emotional issues that affect our daily lives.

*Item #IMAUD    Integrated Movements* ...............*$15.00*

Mail your order (for items on this page only) to:
*Edu-Kinesthetics, Inc., P. O. Box 3395, Ventura, California 93006-3395 USA*
*Telephone or fax order with VISA/MC: Telephone (805) 650-3303 / Fax (805) 650-1689*
*email: EduKBooks@aol.com    website: www.braingym.com*

Prices do not include postage and handling charges. Please add $6.00 for your first item and .75 for each additional item. California residents must add sales tax. Quantity discounts available. Allow three weeks delivery time.

# Jerry Teplitz Enterprises Publications and Products

*All prices are in U.S. dollars.*

**Managing Your Stress: How to Relax and Enjoy** by Dr. Jerry V. Teplitz with Shelly Kellerman

This book is a collection of relaxation techniques covering treatments for everything from headaches and hangovers to migraines and much more.

> *Item #100    Managing Your Stress Book* ...............$15.00

**Switched-On Living** by Dr. Jerry V. Teplitz with Norma Eckroate

This ground-breaking book tells you how to live life to the fullest! It combines proven techniques and the latest research in the body-mind connection using Behavioral and Educational Kinesiology.

> *Item #106    Switched-On Living Book* ...............$15.00

**Travel Stress: The Art of Surviving on the Road** (CD album) by Dr. Jerry V. Teplitz

This exciting six-CD album with workbook is designed to meet the needs of executives, managers, salespeople, and anyone who spends time "on the road." Dr. Teplitz shares with you his proven travel techniques gathered from over 14 years spent traveling as a professional speaker.

> *Item #502    Travel Stress Audio Album* ...............$85.00

**Your Selling Success Formula** (CD album) by Dr. Jerry V. Teplitz

This four-CD album and self-assessment instrument allows you to become a more effective and successful salesperson by understanding your own selling-behavior style as well as your client's buying style. Companies using this program have reported increases in sales of up to 30%.

> *Item #503    Your Selling Success Formula Audio Album* ...............$65.00

**Power of the Mind** (DVD) by Dr. Jerry V. Teplitz

Learn how you can use the power of the mind to accomplish what you want to achieve.

> *Item #602    Power of the Mind DVD* ...............$85.00

**Q-Link Pendant** by Clarus Systems

Electromagnetic pollution (EMP) is around us all the time from lights, TV, and computer screens. It disrupts the integrity and alignment of our own natural field. The *Q-Link* amplifies and activates an EMP-free field around us. The *Q-Link* comes with a 60-day money-back guarantee.

> *Item #011A    Q-Link Black design* ...............$129.00
> *Item #011B    Q-Link White design* ...............$129.00

**Par and Beyond: Secrets to Better Golf** (DVD) by Dr. Jerry V. Teplitz

This hour and ten minute DVD by Dr. Teplitz is a powerful approach for creating a more successful golf strategy than you ever thought possible. It is dynamic, yet practical and shows you tools and techniques that quickly, easily, and immediately put you in charge of developing a winning game. It's a totally different approach from any other golf class you've ever attended. This DVD has been endorsed by Ed Hipp, Golf Coach of the Year, Iowa H.S.

> *Item #041    Par and Beyond: Secrets to Better Golf DVD* ...............$85.00

**Instant Headache and Migraine Relief** (DVD) by Dr. Jerry V. Teplitz

This DVD teaches you a 4,000-year-old Shiatsu (Japanese finger-pressure) technique for pain relief. Both safe and effective, Shiatsu can eliminate a headache or hangover in 1-1/2 minutes, and a migraine in 5 minutes. This DVD also covers sinus colds, stiff necks, and shoulder tension.

> *Item #600    Instant Headache and Migraine Relief DVD* ...............$85.00

Mail your order (for items on this page only) to:
*Jerry Teplitz Enterprises, Inc., 1304 Woodhurst Drive, Virginia Beach, VA 23454 USA*
*Telephone or fax order (800) 777-3529 or (757) 496-8008, Fax (757) 496-9955*
*email: Jerry@Teplitz.com    website: www.Teplitz.com*

To order any of these items go to www. Teplitz.com and click on Books-CDs-DVD or call (800) 77(RELAX). (800) 777-3529. Prices do not include postage and handling charges. Please add $7.00 for your first item and .75 for each additional item. Virginia residents must add sales tax. Allow three weeks delivery time. Dr. Teplitz has a FREE monthly enzine called the Teplitz Email Report. To receive a copy send an email to info@Teplitz.com and type subscribe in the subject line.